GODGROUND

THEE ARRIVAL OF
SAINT MICHAEL

VIC T. FARLEY

Godground: Thee Arrival of Saint Michael
©2021, Vic T. Farley. All rights reserved.
Published by Godground Publishing, Columbus, Ohio

ISBN 978-1-7346229-9-7 (paperback)

Library of Congress Control Number: 2020905521

Website | contact information: Godground.org

DEDICATION

We are all children of God; therefore, this book is dedicated to all of humankind for our struggles, sadness, loss, and the emotional pain that we all feel from time to time as well as to all the victims of hatred (violence), who were once here and are now tragically gone.

God's love—thank God—is something truly beyond great. If we, humanity as a whole, could ever truly be honest with ourselves, God's love is also something that we have all felt somewhere along our road of life. The only question is: Did we allow ourselves to even acknowledge that love?

CONTENTS

PREFACE

This book was sincerely written through divine intervention and it's by means of my philanthropic hopes and prayers that all of humanity shall be taken along their own individual journey through reading this material.

I've known about this book and its material for many years now. There were often times I found myself perplexed from thoughts and struggles considering the many questions that weighed heavily upon me such as: Should this book be taken to my grave for no one to share it with other than God sharing it with me? Or does the good Lord want me to someday publish this material for all the world to see?

Throughout my personal journey with Christ and after many years of deep prayer and a considerable amount of contemplation—along with watching this world changing not for the better—it became distinctively clear that God positively and unequivocally desired this book to be shared with His world. For the marvels of human nature are something exquisitely abundant throughout the globe, and this book is unquestionably for all of you (humanity).

I often felt with great conviction that this was God's plan the entire time. For it was only I who was uncertain in struggling with what to do while safeguarding this material throughout the years. Of the many questions that I asked myself, one of the most profound was: When will this material ever be published?

That time is now.

Please enjoy your journey reading this book and whatever it may bring to you. I earnestly pray that if this book helps only one person, then my job as its humbled author is complete.

You deserve to have your own experience with this book as these words are beyond unique in their cadence as well as their conveyance.

May God bless you throughout everything you venture to seek and find in this life, your adventures, and, of course, in whatever you may choose to read, believe, and be.

Sincerely,

Vic T. Farley

~

CHAPTER ONE

GOD CREATED GOD

There is truly no science regarding God; however, there does exist for all of you (a displaced human race) Godology/Jesusology 101 ideology. And, this book was indeed written for all of you. Whatever you choose to believe, what now follows in all that you (a displaced human race) shall read is for all of humankind to receive: a Godly intervention written through thee God (Jesus Christ's) divine intervention.

Beware, the fourth horse is well on course. Judgment Day is and always was upon all of they (the evil formed through free will that sways against God's way). And, whatever free will you or they (evil) choose, our gods will not refuse. Although foretold throughout countrysides and towns of old, despite their eminent façade mocking thee God (Jesus Christ) with their thorns of skin-torn bloody crowns as Jesus walked upon sand and firth, mankind was well informed—biblically warned in just how to live morally upon Godground (thee earth). When you children of God look above and pray, rest assured God hears all that you say. Ensured as mortals, there are for all morals, a price to pay: Knowing God is also controlling the evil inside hell's repetitious and vicious replay.

God, creator of all that is, whether you perceive or choose to disbelieve, was created by God. God created a beyond-infinitely dividing and gliding autonomous complex energy existing alongside their frameworks of beyond-infinite divine synergy. God does have a complex, because God (thee Father Almighty), our gods, and thee God (Jesus Christ) are beyond-infinitely complex. Thusly, God created our gods (multiple gods) and thee God (Jesus Christ) effectively beyond-infinitely greater than their whole. Nourishing, as well as flourishing, eternally throughout multiple dimensions where there is Godology and Jesusology beyond-infinite realms. This chapter's title serves as its own introduction as you (a displaced human race) briefly pass into Godology/Jesusology 101 ideology.

As this chapter begins unraveling, mankind is also traveling dangerously close to Armageddon's post. Long before God (thee Father almighty) created humankind, God created our gods and thee God (Jesus Christ), your Lord Savior that all of our gods unconditionally favor. As watchers of your sphere, thee God (Jesus Christ) shall make this entire book more than just clear. God's will is done under God's son!

Thee gods are your creators of all that surround you, including hell's repetitive stay, created especially and exclusively just for they (the evil formed through free will that sways against God's way). In being your watchers of Godground existing in a beyond-infinite round—thee arrival of Saint Michael is now upon Godground (your Mother Earth).

Within this book's vibrant Godly cadence, our lords of thee Godsphere, through divine intervention, shall awaken for all of mankind a new understanding delivered through a Christly extension. Our gods also created your biblical antagonist Satan, a simple—although somewhat indicative fictional character—and used to fairly serve free will in your guidance or possibly your defiance.

Before God created the heavens and the earth, God's beyond-infinite gestalt existence created God;

therefore, within God's infinite omnipresence (the quality or state of being present in all places at all times) there is no beginning nor end for you to reference. God (thee Father almighty) formed three externalities of coinciding reality. The first includes an obvious emphasis on God's beyond-infinite realm of absolute genesis, the second a physical world of universal endlessness, and third the soul with its karmic emphasis. Your physical tangible landscapes infinitely divide as well as reshapes. All of thee God's (Jesus Christ's) holy divisions collectively, as well as respectively, form some of God's beyond-omnipotent and beyond-infinite creative precision.

Free of humankind and their censorship of preclusion, thee God (Jesus Christ) shall briefly discuss our God's attribution. God's beyond-infinitely dividing interplay exists within an unapproachable beyond eternal God-complex gestalt realm in a beyond-infinitely directing omnipotent way. God's beyond-infinite inception, developed from within its own beyond-infinite conscious perception: an empowering perpetual life force amid an unending awareness beyond its infinite Godsource. God's beyond-infinite essential pristine nature is an endless and ubiquitous beyond-infinitely dynamic trait. Making God's quintessential Godcore realm, therefore, beyond-infinitely greater than even its beyond-infinite collective summation.

Whereat God is interconnected with all God creates, then obviously each of you (a displaced human race) share a *small* part of these interrelated states. As life emerged a beyond-infinite myriad of frameworks surged throughout—coexisting planes that beyond-infinitely revolve and beyond-infinitely evolve, at the same time merging to become infinitely beyond perfection and grace, arranged. God's multifaceted providence forever rearranges with such rapid complexity; its Godcore summation, therefore, becomes infinitely greater than all of God's creations. Your (a displaced human race's) Big Bang theory and occurrence is clearly a beyond-infinitely Godly divergence (branching out; having no limit). God's omneity created a multidimensional and obviously some parts are tangible—physical reality—God is incapable of being measured by your Big Bang theories of whatever trivial measure. For God's nature of presence is quite noticeably unfettered (beyond-infinitely unrestrained in development).

As thee Godcore arose amid its beyond-infinite enigmatic surge, all life-forms that spawned emerged with such great magnitude and force, moving infinitely beyond your (a displaced human race) god-particle search of source. From within such an unapproachable beyond-infinite God-vitality nexus, no matter the helm, you're (a displaced human race) steering toward an intangible otherworldly realm, making your god-particle quest an even more dangerously alluring nest!

Thee God (Jesus Christ) is intrinsically parts of thee Holy Trinity and goes infinitely *far* beyond your (a displaced human race) theological suitability. Each and every season, mankind deviates further and further from thee God's (Jesus Christ's) biblical bind—harvesting peculiar unreason. Most of your dogmata do have their similar allegiance; nevertheless, too many of them are becoming more abruptly broken across their fundamental regions. There does exist throughout your well recognized and organized religions common threads of belief systems. You (a displaced human race) have become your own carriers within your own doctrines of errors—and by doing so you've created areas of confusion and, at times, disturbing disillusion. It's a direct cause and effect that has taken place by forming various abridged theological material that have, for the most part, become improperly disseminated—shaping and directing confusion regarding God's beyond-infinite ethereal realm. You are leading yourselves into dogmatic dissension with your peculiar continuous religious contention.

God created itself, a beyond-infinitely divine providence that beyond infinitely came into being. Its source created our gods and thee God (Jesus Christ), forming a beyond-infinitely cascading perfection of grace Holy Trinity. Your (a displaced human race's) Catholicism belief system, regardless of your interpretation, is an obvious multiple-Godhead representation.

Consequently, there is a great deal of biblical allegorical (having hidden spiritual meaning that transcends the literal sense of a sacred text) distortion. This has led to your current religious global deflections (a turning aside or off course), resulting in some of their many disturbing and ongoing misdirections.

As a result, your existing Christianity structures have been thrown into a disarray of eluding restructure. These earlier biblical amendments, or censorships, have crossed over from what was once a much brighter and clearer intent and slowly faded into their now blurrier content. Furthermore, by allowing these too many dogmatic redacted divisions, you (a displaced human race) for thousands of years now have succumbed to your own Godly conceptualizing revisions. The original biblical scripting alongside mankind supplementing redacted and censored doctrines have created their own facilitating translations, stripping vast portions of their meaning through your (mankind) intervening causing their many and damaging translations amid much bleaker and shallower notations disturbing those original and intended interpretations.

There are too many examples, especially within your present day, of how mankind continuously finds ample opportunity, for whatever peculiar reasons, in evading God's original scriptural continuity. By composing more than just embellished forms to only contort thee biblical congruity, it's befitting to some extent toward a sorted scriptural mutiny (metaphorically speaking). Thus, through transposing your own Godly-theological elysium (paradise) perspective, you've (a displaced human race) become largely unaware of their many plausible idiom usages—as well as their dialect of varied vernacular directives.

Thee God's (Jesus Christ's) crucifixion served a necessary depiction, however, to believe it was—in any way, shape, or form—some cleverly arranged ransom between God and a devil regarding Adam and Eve, simply further indicates your (a displaced human race) peculiarly growing and overly exaggerated dogmatic gardens of quite peculiar belief.

These perceptions of our gods, no matter thee Trinity, only exemplifies your (a displaced human race's) biblical distortions for truly discerning God's beyond-infinite omnipotent origins. These sorts of Godly-type perceptions are increasingly becoming disconnections from the dogma humankind distorts as you fail to delineate biblical meaning—and yet at the same time—somehow detail these fabricated tales that are misleading. Essentially, your (a displaced human race) religious self-cultivations are developing broken denominations (non-denominations) that secularize people and nations well beyond their intended Christianly formations.

When your vulnerability climbs aboard faithful searches, self-proclaimed prophets do set their shops atop vulture-type perches that dogmatically pander as their profits more than surges. Due to the religion mankind punctures through censorship junctures, it's you (a displaced human race) that now appropriately arrive at another Chapter One juncture— in order to briefly display the obvious similarities of your global theology. This will allow for both an obviously clear juxtaposition as well as its overall current disarray. First and foremost, the many belief systems mankind often clutches to should not allow for moral crutches, too. These moral crutches are often abused; for example, when their followers all too commonly become the judges of other people and their differing beliefs.

As a result of humankind's embellishment, unnecessary redactions, and their censorship involving various artificial adaptions, many of your dogmatic belief systems throughout their passage have become less defined, creating limited discern for you? You (a displaced human race) have already began fading into damaging denominational decline. For this reason, thee God (Jesus Christ) shall reveal small portions surrounding global dogma by separating their distortions and sometimes your complete captive cult alike drama. These many doctrines of dysfunction that exist are nothing more than manmade concoctions that were adopted resulting in an unnecessary paradox among the orthodox. Whether in the name of God or religion, when lives are taken and lands become war-torn, mankind cannot disguise the evil being worn. For your perceived platform of evolution is rapidly becoming a severely and deadly theme of—devolution!

Purgatory begins thee God's (Jesus Christ's) next topic of discussion. For many of you (a displaced human race), this remains a confusing state of mistaken assumption. All of mankind, by design, is prone to sin. It's for this reason that you must try and rethink: What exactly is purgatory? Although

God is not vengeful, there are possibly some forms of forgiveness bestowed upon the many sinful. Once created, your soul shall live forever unless you stray from God's way, shifting into they (the evil formed through free will that sways against God's way). Evil souls are temporarily suspended inside hell's intended nightmare of repetitious despair. There does not exist a rite of passage for they (evil); therefore, the direction you travel throughout the course of your life determines your soul's afterlife. Knowing purgatory is more of an awareness than a state of torment for heavenly preparedness may help.

God created hell, exclusively for they; it's a repetitive loop for all evil spirits and they are now decimated as thee arrival of Saint Michael is upon Godground incarnated. Likewise, hell and its simplistic purpose is and was definitively clear—evil souls, regardless of your (a displaced human race's) presumptions—are not forgiven nor was it ever conveyed they (evil) should be forgiven. God's beyond-infinite nature is too beyond infinitely and inherently all self-preservation—accordingly, this self-preservation ensures evil's decimation. For that's just the way that it is: God is God, and you are just you.

Furthermore, by acknowledging your creator's state of beyond-infinite eternal perfection and grace should only allow you to further understand that God demands the beyond-infinite safeguarding of all that God creates. Commanding ten sent from heaven for all children of God to feed brings to the forefront for all of humankind much to relearn, as Christ's original scriptures inevitably shall return. Evil was never an occupancy of chance nor fate; it's only temporarily created by the free will of morals' vacancy that eventually becomes filled with hate. Heed God's decisive clarity regarding the proceeding verity: A pre-calculated killing of any kind if free will sways untoward, you're impaling only yourself upon that same evil sword.

How absurd bending our Lord's word. For example, an "eye for eye . . . tooth for tooth"—no matter how much you try and soothe, revenge God did *not* ever imply! If an eye is taken from another face, one should reflect: How would you then replace? Of all God's biblical text, this has become the most justified and at the same time unjustified for you (a displaced human race), and when those misinterpretations are upheld, you're indeed taking them totally out of context. It's truly remarkable the hypocrisy that exists within the dogma so many of you choose to rationalize and further twist. When you blindly injure or harm any life that exists in all of God's beyond-infinite magnificent forms, you're unquestionably—at the same time—desecrating and taking away something truly God-born.

As children of God, there are times you may feel abandoned by Christ, or perhaps stranded by your own devices (desire, inclination). You must also attempt to simply understand and trust in God's plan, and that many of our Lord's words you've lost through misinterpretations amid your (a displaced human race) adaptations, inducing for yourselves unnecessary suffocations (to impede or stop the development of). In the outcome, you are suppressing your impending salvation. Free will does indeed serve a divine purpose. However, free will does not exclude the many principles you may willingly fail to affix (to attach or bend), holding you evermore responsible for encroaching on God's commanding fifth (Thou shall not kill).

Gaining nirvana's divine passage is a magnificently long journey of growth the soul amasses, extending well beyond your one lifetime passes. Total spiritual perfection (nirvana) is a pathway, not a title. Only one lifetime would limit the soul by restricting its travel. Reincarnation simply enacts these necessary rehearsal tracks.

The essence of your soul's embodiment, alongside free will and emotional accompaniment, does provide for a necessary balance of elements. These oftentimes become required challenges, and should not be considered a battle, but rather an appropriate segue, to philosophically or symbolically understanding Eve biting the apple. Nothing bad nor evil was ever unleashed from the Garden of Eden: The story was meant to convey the many implications of your free will being set afoot as well as the ramifications of temptations' roots.

Believing in a higher power, all religions stem attempting to flower. Your (a displaced human race) dogmatic expectations are creating secular separations and, in their process, you're also causing yourselves to clash among nations. Even though you're seemingly unaware in the spiritual or religious dichotomy you're choosing to all wear, major religions do share a similar divinity of care. These sorted, albeit similar, indoctrinated divine archetypes that were provided to all of you by God for spiritual growths insight, are becoming hypocritical blows toward other belief systems you choose to either dislike or oppose. The aforementioned shall bring the remainder of Chapter One's attention toward shedding a new light upon your various popular religions. For under God's biblical cover, you (a displaced human race) have been slowly shredding its philosophical and symbolic contents shifting the deeper meaning you need to uncover.

You must truly confess, humankind has created a complete and utter Dogmaplex. Yes?

Current Catholicism conditions endure as well as detour. Many portions of its philosophical purpose eventually resurface through your (a displaced human race's) hypothetical, as well as theological, contradictions. Over time, these mistranslations weakened God's symbolic edifications. Many of your overrepresentations were inadequately deciphered through embellished self-serving folkways and, by doing so, theologically speaking, you've broken away from God's intended pathways. Again, appropriately because of your free will. Moreover, the Holy biblical structure from within its very redacted source gave way to a whole new Christianity infrastructure, fracturing its present course. Christianity from rod-to-reel has become a nondenominational cluster with some groups greatly lacking in their appeal.

Catholicism, as well as its parishioners, is reluctant to distinguish the many obvious scriptural, symbolic messages. In the process, you're (a displaced human race) disabling their true philosophical biblical meaning wherein you also enable a more oppressive (unreasonably burdensome or severe) fable. Your diocese fails to recognize the undeniable Godly relations surrounded by all of God's beyond-infinite nature and creations by fearing their henotheism (the worship of one god without denying the existence of other gods) relations.

Occupied amid thee Holy Trinity exists an obvious multiple-God ideology. If you allow yourselves to see the true essence of thee Holy Trinity, then does it not become noticeably clear as a multiple-godhead of symbolic representation consisting of God (thee Father almighty), Jesus Christ (the son of God), and Christ's Holy Godly Spirit does exist. Therefore, this is a multiple-God depiction. Surrender oneself to the possibility that many scriptures have lost their Godly continuity from their direct effect in your (a displaced human race) neglect and governed authority, and that it was possibly done out of fear for what truly may become uncovered. This shall spearhead for all of humankind the greatest biblical verity (the quality or state of being true or real) and epiphany.

Your Satan is merely a fictional character created by our gods and was intended to exhibit various precautions for all of humankind's appropriate philosophical and symbolic cautions. You have taken God's portrayal of Satan entirely out of context;

the character itself is simply intended for its philosophical concept, and not your non-fictional belief you've somehow processed. Lucifer's discourse, barring your (a displaced human race's) self-created distortion, establishes for all of humankind that when an evil path is freely taken. It shall have a defined course of literally damning proportions.

There are no such fallen (evil) angels. This further exemplifies just how your many symbolic biblical stories are more than capable in moving their readerships as well as the individual interpreter into a myriad of sterner and philosophical tangles. Only you are capable of falling from grace by the careless and deliberate misuse in the profound responsibilities surrounding free will's vast probabilities. For those believing in such nasty devilish gloom, a moment for individual reflection upon if one physically acquired the ability and traveled afar by themselves to the moon, where does this evil truly loom? God, however, is beyond infinite as well as beyond universally in full bloom.

This is quite possibly just how ludicrous some of you've become regarding this fictional character Satan. Due to your beliefs, some will say, the aforesaid is exactly what this fictional character Satan wants you to all believe. Okay. Believe what you want to believe just also understand that God shall continue beyond infinitely throughout eternity being—God. Thee gods created it all, including hell. You may want to appropriately leave those beliefs in Satan to just those that follow Satanism.

Christianity has, over time, peculiarly morphed in its directionality, becoming a nondenomination- ally confusing autonomy. Your (a displaced human race) religious reasons have literally created a con- gregational coliseum (some arranging farce stages) all the while declaring their Christianly engages. Our God's question your sincerity and progression as your many nondenominational segments contin- uously emerge from their misread, self-interpreted, and self-adapted biblical augments.

Polygamist stands are *not* justifiably formed from the holiest strands. Its precisely these types of distorted beliefs that merely exemplify your self-created missions hidden (in guise) behind their self-manufactured biblical renditions, leading many Godly good Christians deeper into a very peculiar and disturbing moral contradiction. Mankind is continuously developing misguided religious per- ceptions that are merely breeding newer and far greater divine digressions.

Moreover, these various congregational move- ments are not improvements, but are simply auton- omous sectional units that slowly, over time, have taken themselves biblically apart. Throughout this endless process of tossing about God's biblical index, you have once again taken large portions of scriptures out of context ever so inappropriately, arranging your (a displaced human race) variety tone from their already-overgrown glossing (to mask the true nature of) syntax. These assorted and contorted dissections of Christianity have some synthetically developing in wayward directions. Replacing thee hallow-filled roads with monetary gains well-suited for their proprietors to entertain—pontificating amid gilded uncurbed lanes.

Some of your organized Christian affiliations use, as do many others, religiosity for its welcoming commodity all the while restructuring theology into a more unorganized hypocrisy quality. As some establishments charge your (a displaced human race's) television dramas toward funding their rising megachurches that have some being veiled (in a sincere roundabout way) behind million-dollar organizations surreptitiously, attempting to sincerely appear as if their being, holier upheld. Some of them hide inside their revenue fields as establishments spring forth their fountains of accountants and in the process. Some are complacently displaying for God their blatant pandering parvenu. When spreading the gospel perhaps it's not best to buy private jets from the donations you request?

Christianity's original nexus has morphed into excess, offering too many cornucopias of belief systems to address, making any attainable and salvational access an incredibly copious process. These myriads of redemptive panaceas within many of your dogmatic beliefs are causing more confusion than it is relief.

Our gods suggest for all of humankind that you try not to religiously obsess and perhaps instead allow yourselves to reassess the marvels of all life and the true nature of God's beyond-infinite blessings surrounding your days and nights. Knowing God is oftentimes an individual as well as a shared journey and shall provide all the growth necessary for you in this life and your afterlife's entry. Too many belief systems suffer from their assorted and, at times, thwarted self-manufactured and drastic prerequisites and unnecessary strictness. Their witnesses are merely becoming the results of their own misinterpreted readerships that structure converted gospel trips.

Far too many of you (a displaced human race) are truly good Christian followers; however, as you search for a salvational cure you are also subjecting yourselves to the many masquerading false prophets' and faith healers' entertaining lure. These games are too often played amid their many biblical charades that hide behind ulterior, although at times this may be sincere, shades. Some establishments chomp at the bit to sell miracles behind rehearsals read from their teleprompting scripts. Our gods question how far reaching are these contributions? Perhaps there should be more visible solutions? As their members' donations spree, what worlds are changing outside these organizations partaking for themselves in such luxury with their attached chauffeur-driven fees?

There are many of you Godly good Christians on viable missions although you've created a peculiar overflow congregationally, consisting of extremely differing biblical renditions denominationally. God's concerns lie within your (a displaced human race's) deviating biblical accounts and their many twisted turns that were in vast amounts written for their symbolic as well as philosophic terms—and not necessarily always from actual accounts.

It's imperative for all of you to firmly understand a global religion comparative does exist—no matter their brand. Too many of your denomination builders have been supported throughout their bolstered pillars by their own induced fear that produced a desire to steer others away from any and all conceivable polytheistic material of nature. Hebrew translations inevitably failed because of their many idiomatic migrations that eventually became distributed through their altered censorship and their various interpretations.

Some of your Christian theology collections are too commonly becoming more established through their internal and external obsessions—all the while you're overlooking their much more practical and simplistic lessons. Does, for example, God's love not shine upon the poorest of those souls that are unable to attend service because their surrounded by an impoverished surface? Will God punish those who do not believe in Jesus Christ although many of these people are relatively living a morally good life? Even though their belief system for you (individually) is not right? If a child dies not knowing God or Christ, does God truly forsake that soul? If so, at what price? Whatever God may require, surely does not include a specific choice of ecclesiastical attire. If that were the case here, another moment for reflection: Who's right and who's wrong? God shall decide that one. Each of you should earnestly reach inside yourselves to help question what it is you truly require in order to acquire, a direction toward improving your desired spiritual and moral growth progression. And, perhaps some of you should just stop using religion as a shield only to seek refuge inside some of your arenas filled with hypocrisy, where ultimately nothing is concealed from God (thee Father almighty).

Some Islam submissions and the ignorance therefrom are creating undiscerningly peculiar misunderstandings and glare from, too many people that are only able to identify Islamic belief systems by those who tear its very holier foundation through their more radical (violent and hateful) formation. What about the other millions of Islamic followers that are living harmoniously throughout the world? Islam is a peaceful belief system in its origin and essence. Other religions have suffered similar forms of radical tainting whenever their believers become evermore extreme by rearranging an interpretation to better fit their personal (individual) motivation. These misled radical interpretations lead to Quran deviations. These types of dangerous motions travel in tides across oceans, creating unnecessary dissension from within your numerous dogmatic incomprehension. Your (a displaced human race's) Islamic contortions (to twist in a violent manner) blind their revealing and similar worldwide theological devotions (the belief in God, heaven, hell, and judgment). An unfortunate example for all of you concerning the radical tainting that occurs throughout other belief systems is realizing that some followers (individuals) of other belief systems have killed doctors for performing abortions.

When some of you (a displaced human race) begin distorting divine meaning by inappropriately shifting their peaceful narratives, the few unprincipled causes exceeding Quran clauses develops for the Islamic faith—ever-dangerous optics of preconceived opinions and prejudice, producing an eclipsing tolerance in the West. Some Muslim (very few overall) radical (violent and hateful) partite cells stifle their obvious truer peaceful Islamic solidarity veils. God repels your unholy wars that only they (the evil formed through free will that sways against God's way) attempt to dogmatically ascribe outside of what the Quran or Hadith truly represent. It's only wherefrom and is quite beyond ignorance that so many misinterpretations cause the bending of interpretations that eventually tend to collide.

Wars' manifestations are born only of humankind confrontations and bear *no* holy affiliations. When evil implications are silhouetted deceptively around religious contempt or within governments of discontent, it's from God that you've become disconnected.

"Warriors" who portray their evil deeds under the unholy guidance outside Quran/Hadith alliance, and only in guise, are being committed in vain. They are ungodly Jannah (Muslim concept of heaven or paradise) pursuits that end beneath hell's deepest roots. Your (a displaced human race's) Jihad struggles have become nothing more than extreme dogmatic shuffles wherein: The unholy wars they (the evil formed through free will that sways against God's way) rage are only torn from evil's page. These wars too often use religion and peaceful belief systems for a nefarious masquerade.

Gods do not create nor engage in wars. Your Aztec Empires vanished, practicing outside similar ungodly wards. Soldiers beckon suicidal recruits— Hadith to Quran doctrines—only they (evil) pollute.

Buddhism teachings are far more philosophically reaching. From its true Buddhavacana-natured Core, all life our gods create must endure growth alongside your own fate. The liberation you're seeking is a journey easier traveled once you begin to realize your life as well as your being coexist to reveal the freeing you're seeking. Souls are philosophically similar to your bodhi tree branches— through inherent nature and desire for advances— growing in different directions, supplying your individual connections. Believing you're truly suffering is not the healthiest perspective for nirvana's uncovering.

Reincarnations have their afterlife foundations. Barring Buddhism from your religious institutions in fear of its canonical intrusions leaves far too many with empty and alarming philosophical seclusion. No matter what proof you dogmatically seek, the four noble truths are an optional pragmatic peak. If your physical being had an impervious covering for all its suffering, knowing no loss, then you may never seek the many roads upon those divine noble paths' that lay across (as to find or meet) inside all of your God provided (Catholicism, Christianity, Judaism, Islam, Hinduism, Buddhism, and Godology/Jesusology 101 ideology) walks.

Hinduism's theism and its nonconformist belief system captures the essence of tolerance, a profound element unfortunately absent at times, throughout too many belief systems and religious involvements. Within its polytheism diversity, there lies a great deal of versatility for the individuals' journey as life strands unfold purposely. However, through such Hinduism/Buddhism directions, you're unrealistically forming connections to suffering as a condition that must be endured to find truer meaning. Nevertheless, when you choose to identify that the essence of karma is a relative trait for your way of life, you will begin to realize that without your current state of physical presence and being there would not exist the desired paths for reincarnation nor karma's meaning.

Creedal emphasis appropriately surrounds a divine genesis, understanding Hinduism's expansiveness opens a celebration for karmic expressiveness. Gender regulations throughout Muslim and Hindu generations have indeed greatly disregarded the female significance. It's these very types of indifferences that create afterlife and karmic consequences. This again defines the dogma ambivalence within humankind's revolving belief systems that too many times lead to an immense antithesis. In other words, God created both your female and male significance. Yes? Or did God only create the man?

Echelons built amid the hilt of worshiping pantheons, do not mold your individual transmigrations through social caste arrangements. Karma is a magnificent journey for the soul to amass, yet carries *no* significance amid your social class. It's neither a blueprint nor guise for any belief system to individually decide what types of people to then socially chastise.

Judaism monotheism movements awaiting messianic redemption do appropriately, as well as accordingly, receive thee God (Jesus Christ's) complete exoneration from all biblical crucifixion—ludicrously *false* accusations. These very dangerous types of interpretations exemplify the common variations that have occurred throughout scribing fabrications only to become total threads of separation. Your (a displaced human race) critical interpretations and misled biblical translations have taken what was once originally inscribed for mankind into its present form—breaking apart its scriptural continuity, leaving far too many pieces of ambiguity.

Philosophical versus symbolical interpretations are exactly what widen the many biblical seams that have, over time, developed into their more retracted, also redacted, and peculiarly dangerous interpretations. Resulting in humankinds' scriptural decline as well as some of your overall incline for insensible reasoning. Thee God (Jesus Christ's) Mother Mary was Jewish. Yes. This should be obvious for all of you, unfortunately it's not. Again, perhaps refer back to, the back cover of this book—thee gods are becoming disenchanted with many of humankinds' troubling issues. If you (the individual reader) had no idea that thee God (Jesus Christ) was indeed Jewish, then you have some research to do.

Your Middle Eastern clashes are more troubling examples of the complete hypocrisy and very peculiar behavior mankind attaches toward the process within both your heavenly pursuits alongside their battleground disputes. As you fight over the wrongs versus rights, your differing faiths dilutes their more than obvious similar pursuits (God). When you're blinded by the similarities of divine pages, you (a displaced human race) form philosophical cages as readerships oftentimes allow Old Testaments to bring New Testaments ever further away from their significantly related pages.

Gaza strips enlist their own scourging credo splits. The Eastern biblical inversions that open Hamas's violent insurgence display for God the highest forms of holy divergence. God's earth was divinely given and shall only become united through humankinds' peaceful vision.

These are distinctive warnings for you (a displaced human race) and your incessant warring shall bring forth God's extinctive storming. Palestinians forming terrorism dominions within their politically driven and religious dissensions shall fall by the sides of a new ascension.

Although two-state alternatives carry their own conflicts of interest, it can also facilitate their many irreconcilable differences. Insincere political rides weaken your (a displaced human race) strides. It's from this very combination that you form your own diverging confrontations that inevitably emotionally collide with wars' opposing sides. Whether biblical or Nakba, these cyclical disputes and plaguing exodus routes can eventually have their reconcilable roots.

No matter the platform, there is *no* forum for the violence and hatred that has poured through the East. As they (the evil formed through free will that sways against God's way) terrorize the East and West with bombs upon evil's chest, these too many conflicts surrounding your belief systems that should be uniting humankind and not fighting mankind shall soon become one god-eclipsing rest!

~

CHAPTER TWO

YOU (A DISPLACED HUMAN RACE)

God's love for each and every one of you (a displaced human race) is pure and, therefore, justly incomprehensible. God's (thee Father almighty's), our gods', and thee God's (Jesus Christ's) love is an extension beyond your comprehension. In knowing that you are children of God, thee Father almighty's entire omniscience (infinite knowledge and awareness), as well as God's perfection and grace, is filled with a love and desire that transcends for you an unfathomable benevolence throughout and beyond all of God's provenance.

You (a displaced human race) have by no means been forsaken nor misplaced. Your life does have a significant purpose as well as meaning. Your free will, that God has so graciously bestowed upon all of you, also has its greatest share of responsibility and care.

Being aware of what is truly right or wrong requires little biblical scrutiny. Creating Satan's fictional character simply allowed for all of you to further understand and develop that immense responsibility residing inside free will's two-path probability. One must be cautious in all that free will manages to yield. For free will may be used to build or destroy, however you choose to wield it. Many of you are taking your lives much too seriously, while many others are failing to understand their actions are reactions that carry a magnitude of severity.

As a displaced human race, you must first begin working steadily on softening your pace. Technological advancements have ignited, causing mankind to become overly accelerated and artificially invited as you also grow progressively more divided. These immense digital highways are merely creating denser byways, paving their way toward unstable and faster pathways—a pivotal self-evaluation not to be ignored. Silicon Valleys have opened many essential alleys; these gates were Godly opened, although their purpose has become inevitably violated. Historically, you have developed a considerable propensity for biting the apples of curiosity.

Your social media gatherings are becoming exceedingly less flattering, filled with their electronic posts and decadent facial overbooked gloats, drowning in text you're barely treading in context. Overloaded stimuli artificially tie your attractions, effecting further distractions away from Godly abodes, driving you precariously toward innocent lives that swiftly shift down fractured roads. Grabbing smartphones of enslaving art forms, you're selfishly creating larger gaps within your family tracks. Be wary in that precious time does often vary as well as quickly elapse due to your many apps being downloaded upon isolated laps that have become timely and numb baited traps. This overactivity reduces your humility as you reach for more and more accessibility all the while diminishing your inner peace and tranquility.

Your personal enchantments, alongside their exploding technological advancements, were once again Godly provided for all of you for the sole purpose of serving and furthering your altruistic enhancement. These information networks that were intended to simplify your reality instead cause unwise and disguised overwork throughout your societies, increasing your needs as you also decrease and deteriorate your personal well-being. Many prior civilizations have advanced all too rapidly and have greatly suffered from their newly found alchemy (a power or process that changes or transforms something in a mysterious or impressive way). These technological changes have severely inundated mankind disrupting your behavioral and moral patterns. Heed this warning that hides inside your displacement and rearrangement of behavioral and moral patterns—all that you technologically alter bring unforeseen and new responsibilities that you must also foster.

Failing to control going down the digital rabbit hole may lead you into a great deal of unanticipated chain reactions causing unwanted events of your own actions. All that you seek to research and develop of your own accord, may in the long run envelop a mounting cost that humankind cannot afford. God encourages your growing prudent curiosity as its presence helps acquire for humanity many suitable developments; however, those beyond your earthly odyssey are being monitored respectively. As your curiosity grows, remain mindful in all the possible directions your many paths may eventually disclose.

Beware of your free will and its presence, as its essence is always at play, and acknowledge its ever-changing role carries a toll. As you begin moving toward brighter Godground connections, you shall access and safeguard against free will's wayward directions. Live your life as you see befit nevertheless; understand it's truly a gift. It's wise to remain aware just how far from God you (a displaced human race) may at times drift.

There are obviously actions as well as reactions that accompany your free will; therefore, one must duly regard these significant corresponding relations without disregarding their indicative contemplations. Bear in mind the impact your free will carries daily, let alone in just one lifetime, as you consider what exactly you are choosing because you are also free to adapt. Moreover, the footprints you leave behind pack more than just earthy imprints when your free will acts; their impressions inevitably press forward as karma tracks.

Within your earthy grips, a simple glimpse of your history reveals just how often humankind quickly slips into war's misery. These incessant conflicts, as you build and then destroy, surely contradict your many perspectives within all of your worldwide religious directives.

Many assorted caveats throughout this book are being purposefully brought to your attention; it's best these do not become overlooked. Various changes await your displaced human race. This book is meant to expand your comprehension and not necessarily compound your apprehension. You're increasingly becoming a threat to one another alongside Mother Nature; by ignoring these afore-mentioned Godground caveats then humankind shall not have time to regret as Godground may very well become an evolutionary reset. The wars born amid evil's hateful tear shall not pass through the Godground exosphere, scraping through God's infinite galaxies of universal care.

Moreover, rest assured that our gods are closely watching your celestial allure. Mankind shall always stay well grounded, as the wars from whence they (the evil formed through free will that sways against God's way) are mounted shall never travel to become unearthly routed. As for your proverbial hindsight being twenty-twenty, it's your lack of truly learning from such a vast past of bloody history that man-kind should never fail to properly restudy.

Although your space exploration programs may have some of your researchers riveted, your tech-nologies remain for many reasons extremely primi-tive, keeping your (a displaced human race's) atmo-spheric obstruction and destruction closely limited. The greed and need that mankind constantly exhib-its shall also remain Godground restricted as other planets and moons are prohibited from the devastation caused by too many excavations. The geological disruption brought forth through the many years of free will eruption (the sudden occurrence or appearance of) shall never be tolerated beyond earth's irruption!

All that you may ever need shall always be provided for you by God (thee Father almighty). Regardless of what you think you need this will not necessarily coincide with what God divinely sees befitting your individual needs.

Temptations and their many difficult contemplations greatly disturb your moral evaluations at times. If you succumb to your temptations through justifying your selfish motivations, many unforeseen complications shall arise from your false gratification.

Your self-gratification is a temporary pleasure sensation wherein you need to acquire a greater self-examination of your individual satisfaction. As such, these considerations surrounding temptations shall oftentimes have their many moral deviations that manipulate the outcome, making it perhaps more difficult for you to overcome.

Your (a displaced human race's) lust carries its own gust of wayward temptations; these seductive free will deviations only lead to further corrupting your significant loving relations. Once you bring such lust into your forefront, all that you desire may become an ever-darker hunt set dangerously a spark only to then catch fire. Whereupon you also begin losing your sight amid the immorality you no longer struggle with nor fight.

The reeling from your stealing winds itself through many wayward roads that all too often only become winding and unappealing. Whatever your consciousness deals in justifying all that you now need to conceal does not rectify the injustice covering your morality misdeal. Carrying all that you covet in your chase toward reaching a much higher summit eventually turn into morally unbalanced precipices further weighted by your immorality that may only continue to plummet. Be mindful of the justifying and rationalizing within your consciousness for there may be no chance of changing its course within your free will acts, becoming your own vessel assail without a mast.

Inside whatever you may feel that you lack upon your paths, one can always with faith know that God's love for you shall always outlast. Regardless of what you truly feel this life has cast unto you, each of you are simply experiencing your individual growth the soul must amass.

This materialistic world that too many of you so ardently adore are becoming increasingly occupied spaces of extravagant hoard. Success *does* become a much more profound prevalence wherever it's sincerely displayed through the virtues of altruism and benevolence—and *not* your overindulgence. The stairs at the foot of opulent altars gather a great deal of greed that only falters as so many people squander; meanwhile, the poor and needy are being denied as the less fortunate continue suffering. God is now uncovering for all of you (a displaced human race) that thee heavens above have also cried right beside you. One nourishes the soul through the hands of philanthropy in order to provide for the plenty, whereas at the hands of overindulging materialistically, one is fed individually and ever so avariciously.

The blessed Godground—that humankind is merely leasing—is on the verge of becoming a discarded wasteland as your devolution is unleashing an ever-increasing appetite for drugs, violence, adulterated sex, and the pollution of por*n*ography.

Other cultures have perished with their remnants of similar Godground neglect buried under shore—as you read do not just ignore. Your carbon footprints are becoming proliferating plastic implants intruding upon nature's den. Mother

Nature's increasing clash with your discarded waste throughout oceans amid aquatic life are suffering in their motion, and have now become greatly entangled by your failure to foretaste its ecological crash. Thee Godground you're neglecting has already begun showing signs of naturally rejecting, as mankind is not truly seeing that you're being washed under by its own looming ocean flowing backlash.

Earth is home for all of God's creatures to freely nest as well as roam; this delicate relationship among nature you must by no means continue to disown.

Your ecosystems are displaced, in that mankind has chased too many species into extinction, disturbing nature's delicately balanced distinctions. The bloody carcasses that many are poaching and selling through black markets for nothing more than their avarice wins are evermore compelling (demanding attention) Godground-encroaching sins.

God has reserved a special hierarchy for all animals upon Godground, whereby you are not the dominator of this shared and Godly declared territory. Animals truly deserve the love, care, and respect that humanity is more than capable of providing, and their well-being are absolutely your (a displaced human race's) complete dominion of responsibility. Eat what you harvest just as you harvest how you reap. Are there no other alternatives for humankind other than the animal slaughtering you seek?

The rainforests you're uplifting are due to the reins of mankind over-gripping and forfeiting too many of your future alternatives. As a result of your own campaign of careless and recklessly free climatically clipping and destroying your Godground forests and trees, you're unable to see the forest because there are fewer and fewer leaves. The dawn of your many wooded inlands have now drawn into unhooded and barren cyclical wastelands. Your deforestation has long been breached and it's already reached humankind's ability to repair thee Godground stability including your polluted air.

The ecological disruptions that you are and have been experiencing that befall humankind's construction, are only mild introductions from your own affects and once again your environmental neglects are the result of self-designed earthly interruptions. Glaring erosions to baring the frozen, Mother Nature's delicate grove is becoming dangerously unwoven. By disturbing these atmospheric motions, mankind is only increasingly flirting with nature's devotion. Averting further catastrophic anomalies must be done through curbing your geological ferocity and slowing earth's destruction, ecologically speaking.

Animal habitats and their precious fabric through which mankind is tearing eventually revert back in the direction of all life-forms surrounding their bearing. Raising the earth's thermostat through your obtrusive infrastructure of artificial restructure only reveals the many unseen atmospheric gaps. It is possible that humankind is writing its own epitaph by writing off too many habitats. Is mankind ready, willing, and able to begin more resolving and less devolving? Your struggles and neglected oversight in coexisting with nature are only pushing the odds acre by acre further away from your favor.

Once these intricate landscape fabrics become too unsown, their covers uncover to shake nature's very cornerstone. Affording yourselves all the luxuries that you've built may surprisingly become a despairing cost—Mother Nature's price may be to tilt!

You're deafening the sound of wilderness calls by your ever-increasing timber hauls that are leaving precious wildlife stranded and abandoned as nature cries out—God listens to all of their shouts. This distress thrusted upon the wilderness as a direct result of your intrusive ingress at Mother Nature's access is also allowing the uncovering that increases the soils dampness, causing the many mudslides that smother your awareness.

From inside your many wide and gaping photosynthesis voids leaves unrest and difficulty for the gathering of abounding and necessary elements that are required for balancing your surrounding environments. These disastrous ecological displacements shall only worsen the more you fail to address this developing dangerous imbalance. As you further contest planet earth, humankind must learn to stop challenging its elegantly delicate nest.

Moreover, your environmental problems as well as your depletion of resources shall only compound throughout their courses. This is your cause and effect from what humankind directs toward being too many times self-appointed and many more times undevoted alongside thee Godground you've left unkept!

At your current alarming rates, humankind is invariably sealing its own fate. Your "going green" is not stopping on red, ignoring all the warning signs upon Mother Earth that you've too far bled. What was once hinging is now beyond hemorrhaging: Caution abounds in your race ahead. Mankind may not outlast its own ecosystem forecast. Furthermore, if the damage upon Godground continues of that mankind inflicts, Mother Nature sooner or later evicts.

Oceans are inappropriately churning arising from your waste; these shorelines are appropriately returning, rising above your waist. All the waste and pollution mankind set free now suffocates marine biology as you (a displaced human race) slowly strangle and entangle everything at sea. Elevated temperatures amid the Godground you've breached are scarring the ocean's floor, fated to be coral reefs that now lie tainted and bleached.

Your coastal impacts of marine habitats are drowning in toxic waste spilled from your crude oil mistakes. Biodiversity transformations are rapidly shifting into more oceanic degradations, only moving yourselves into plausible and *contingent* Godground eviction.

You (a displaced human race) have always been temporarily placed upon thee Godground space. There does exist for you a cyclical reality that's recurring; the morality you continuously fail to capture eventually further descends and therefore rewrites your final chapter. Your history once again reveals many compelling and telling stories of humankinds perished civilizations as well as their various uncivilized immoral operations.

Free will is another contributing and recurring abovementioned factor, which provides for mankind endless options; however, by God allowing its full rein, you (a displaced human race) usually too easily become your own incarcerator and captor. Living on thee Godground surface requires all its occupants to live in a Godly service. Failing to acknowledge this apparent obligation is precisely what alters your entire course of plausible reclamation (to bring back to a preferable manner of living, sound principles, ideas, etc.).

Fate unfolds unto whatever morality humanity beholds. Whenever the foundation of morality degrades, and its fundamentals are no longer upheld, your immoral paradigms begin to extremely shift. This sets the eminence of mankind adrift into a reckless course of Godly recourse (a source of help, strength, or protection).

This rampant decay within your moral breakdown is becoming more prevalent as each decade turns around. Throughout the lineage of your human race, there has never existed such an actively rapid moral decline when relatively paired with all the knowledge humanity collectively has and whenever it's sincerely shared. The presence of your moral breakdown has only grown to become increasingly infringed upon alongside the more you're shown.

Once your essential moral principles and values become unhinged, it can only lead to the many now living amid its moral fringe.

Humankind unto morality's decline grows into its own individual resolution when it's unwaveringly seated throughout every moral seed that too many of you are failing to firmly plant over time. Abilities for distinguishing what outlines right from wrong are rapidly becoming faded lines among an increasingly jaded humankind. Undeniably concerning is your failure to acknowledge the many consequences of your immoral offenses that appear to be growing in their onset alongside your lack of regret—furthering your course that has for some become distantly absent of remorse.

Through misusing the powers of your free will that God (thee Father almighty) has so graciously and lovingly bestowed upon each and every one of you, by way of justifying and rationalizing your immoral acts only gives rise to the possibility for the many unwise to continue fostering down their self-altering unethical paths. To help yourselves guide and reduce your immoral strife (an act of contention: fight or struggle) you must understand there does exist a meaning and purpose for your (individual) life. Likewise, just one person's precious life can have an enormous impact on all other life based solely upon their Godly bestowed free will as well as their moral integrity inside their (individual) principles of valued path.

The many problems that continue to plague humanity are directly affected through the bending of morals some of you (a displaced human race) fail too many times to clearly define. Throughout each passing generation, there does exist an overlapping moral decline. Humanity's devolutionary course has become considerably disenchanting throughout many years now. Morally you're deteriorating, all the while you're immorally accelerating.

Knowing your right from wrong as well as what is good-versus-evil behavior is definitively not an element that only belong to whomever identify themselves as biblically or religiously strong. You are also natured by God and you're supposed to be nurtured through families, friends, and school to ensure these tremendously basic principles are carried along. This crucial nurturing component is another significant aspect within your free will itself.

There is a growing morality dysfunction that again appears ever increasing as too many of your basic morals, principles, and values are decreasing alongside your full rein of free will. Thee God (Jesus Christ) is reminding humankind to stay mindful of this indeed. These are clear warning signs of your many unsteady and problematic ever-changing times. Humankind should perhaps reassess, as you live in your now days, and recall the rest of do-you-remember when days?

Your morals and codes are becoming more and more vacant roads that humankind must *not* fail to improperly address. In knowing your temptations and greed can both easily pull to attract too many fools, therefore, mislead—these aforesaid reflections may help the indiscretions humankind cannot disguise nor hide from God (thee Father almighty). Far too many times even the wise become misled by the many unwise that have led.

The possession of free will can falsely empower your morality discretions whereas controlling one's free will does become a power that's best upheld through your individual determination. When properly used, or perhaps abused, your individual abilities are either the leader or the follower.

Do bear in mind that it's okay for you to portray yourself both as the leader and the follower. For each of you throughout your life have followed something and, therefore, have also become led by that something. Indiscretions can easily become progressions that alter your morality directions. Applying your own rationale regarding indiscretions may intensify other improprieties for you and their transgressions.

Unity within families, faith, and neighboring communities are progressively displaced as your human race develops too many broken homes and emptier plates. Your primordial desires are increasingly appearing, and not necessarily coinciding, with your responsibilities that only individually you can employ and hire. Some of you are childbearing with such great ease at the same time; some of your childrearing comes with absolutely no guarantees.

Children are bearing children to foster homes that too many times only provide temporarily shelter and further disunion, all the while many of these children are desperately searching for their own family reunion. There is a direct effect and unseen repercussions inside and outside your many family separations as your unfortunate lack of unity disrupts more than emotional and moral continuity.

These disconnections of various unity bring forth for much of humanity many unforeseen indirections. For philosophical reflection regarding the unity of wildlife and human offspring: If all animals were to abandon their unity, which is not possible, their species would cease to exist, making life itself, whether it's domesticated or undomesticated, utterly meaningless. Consequently, union in itself is a naturally born primary element that surrounds every aspect of life and its precious development. Unity feeds the essence within all primordial human needs and also parts of the many themes are present throughout your bountiful Godly given creeds.

Racism, regardless of your displaced rationalism, is precisely the ingredient (a quality or characteristic that makes something possible) that gave rise to the fascism of Nazi Germany, which was used in evil attempts to exterminate thee Jews. This, unfortunately, is a horrid example of just how such a union can also assemble and form itself into a nefarious restructure of disunion, driven by hatred and accelerated by a racist supremacist twisted ideology. They (evil) are guilty on God (thee Father almighty) scales of final justice that infinitely outweigh; all evil spirits are decimated that were once in hell, repetitiously incarcerated.

Recognize and examine that your displaced rationalism in regards to racism can easily erupt and, therefore, be used to temporarily form a union that in every aspect is simply a total façade for a corrupt and darker disunion. Racist groups are nothing more than hateful troops unified in a movement to rationalize, through finding and exposing those weaknesses in others only for their selfish benefit of charging (to rush against or attack) by evil

inducement. Your human race is growing evermore
displaced wherein your contention within all racial
brands rise to become extremely precarious stands
upon thee Father almighty—Godground lands.
Understand there is no real black or white hidden behind your racism fight. No matter your color,
in failing to love one another through creating dissension that spearheads racial tension eventually
uncovers only one communal shed of lineage and
color: bloodshed! Embracing your differences shall
only expedite the development humanity respectively requires to acquire. By shunning alike species, you're stunting the growth humans inherently
desire for sharing in the joys of simply being different and not seeing someone necessarily as ethnically
different. Whether you choose to believe in reincarnation or choose to ignore this following reflection
that may be a revelation. Perhaps your soul returns
to live embodied in a racially diverse relation?

Hypocrisy, at times, can allow for its own sorted
spiritual mockery (by individually and philosophically reflecting upon) and unfortunately hypocrisy
is becoming a more prevalent form of behavior.
Unfolding throughout some of humanities congregations, inside the many different denominations
you continue to organize. It's vital that humankind understands that by using hypocrisy in order

to manipulate your beliefs for yourself and others, you're simply masquerading, temporarily, your sinful deceits. If you find yourselves just going through the formalities of unspiritual motions, perhaps you should refine the self through attempting to be clearer within your individual devotions.

Your displaced Godly devotion is becoming a rippling effect that has been creating a great deal of confusion and way too much commotion for many of you (a displaced human race). This is exactly whereby religious cults gain their prolific and dangerously insincere, nefarious motion. Whereat you (children of God) and those who once worshipped only to die miserably in a mass murder of suicide at the people's temple, thee God (Jesus Christ) did observe, as well as reserve a special hell for its temple founder.

The expectations that one may have in searching for their answers from a higher power should never lead anyone to *adorn* another mortal man or woman claiming to be healing others by God's command, especially if the number of their followers are smaller than thee God's (Jesus Christ's) Godground acknowledgers. Such false prophets are serving their own delusional plan and are doing so upon Godground land. Religious cult movements are usually made from their leaders distorted biblical routes as they (evil) sit high atop only serpents' mount. God bestows freedom as well as free will; it's ungodly for any such freedoms to ever become repressed by those false prophets attempting to create such unrest.

Whether these religious cults are gathering in open Buddha fields or hidden behind barricades of Branch Davidian-pandering biblical charades, such false prophets—and always with a friendly demeanor—are merely practicing from well-planned tactics used to conceal their evil ulterior. These religious cult leaders and their unkept promises weave for their devoted followers a healing or spiritual journey for only their *chosen* ones to see, as it gradually leads to a more twisted and sadistic ominous decree.

What some of you reference to be your religious preference or a missionary filled with reverence, are nothing more than religious cults filled with a dangerous visionary presence. Many religious cults are organized to inspire as they (the evil formed through free will that sways against God's way) gather followers with impulsive hearts beating across a disheartening salvation pulse. Some of you are taking as well as breaking central dogmatic fundamentals by creating exalting ensembles of ludicrous principles and practices that are meaningless additives.

Through the belief systems some of you've hyp-
ocritically fed as well as biblically bled, from their
uses and their too many abuses of religion for its
financial and emotional gains, have more than
become their own organized religions of unorganized divisions. Attempting to alleviate what,
exactly, is it that pains some of you? Are these personal financial, tax-exempt pains, materialistic, or
perhaps both? Christianity is now suffering its own
separation and confusion because of its never-end-
ing fusion of nondenominational clusters.

If our gods required any of you to uphold your
many stringent and cogent doctrines, not one of
you would ever make it to heaven—nor would any
of you even be remotely capable in achieving any
form of atonement or spiritual well-being. Religion
is not a business in which, as its witness, you restrict
and therefore strip the freedoms as well as the free
will of others from simply rejoicing. Perhaps there
is a fear that if this was not done, some people may
become too spiritually invigorated?

In your many searches to discover God and
to uncover where exactly it is you belong, you're
becoming too easily charmed and blindly deceived
by the allure of false prophets and their pandering dogma concoctions—alongside their entertaining doctrines for profits. Your endless rules and

regulations regarding forgiveness and salvation are only creating for some of you many unrealistic expectations. Furthermore, many of your religious affiliations are forming more contradicting denominations and, by doing so, some of you are creating dogmatically peculiar disputes and too much bickering that've already become more deadlier feuds.

Faith offers for each and every one of you so much more other than just hope. It also allows you to open your mind and hearts for that necessary connection of your (individual) and exclusive celebration of enhancing spiritual growth. Additionally, by creating that much needed personal divine connection inside the guidance you receive of your individual faith and belief systems benefits your personal Godly reflection and that relationship that only you (individually) can have with God.

The guidance that each of you receive within your faith and beliefs is not something that will be necessarily instantly perceived, it's more of an awareness through your personal and individual relationship with God that all of what you seek eventually is received. Free will does not necessarily imply full rein, nor is God's beyond-infinite domain over all creations made in vain.

There is life infinitely beyond your carbon base, with alternative realities extending infinitely further than your Milky Way space. Many are carried amid light waves, hiding aboard hues of shimmering infinite velocity—traveling well beyond your humankind avenues of odyssey. Lunar shadows and their fractured light afterglows cast unique realms of energy. Their structured motion exists within an alternate existence of infinite activity.

Your too many conflicts stretch beyond to many continents and you (a displaced human race) remain unaware of their unseen consequences as you erase to quickly pass the significance of humankind history. No matter their cause, your displaced wars are only opened through evil hands that hatefully applaud. Upon Godground, they and only they (the evil formed through free will that sways against God's way) are creating your endless battlegrounds. These are meaningless slaughters wherefrom God (thee Father almighty), our gods, and thee God (Jesus Christ) silently monitors for all of mankind, and are more than becoming for all of you (a displaced human race) progressively dangerous waters.

God (thee Father almighty), our gods, and thee God (Jesus Christ) are becoming increasingly disenchanted by thee Godground humankind is taking for granted. Whenever evil dares to cast hatreds anchorage, miraculously it's only temporary dockage. The peace God inevitably charters envelops to indelibly provide harbor. These avarice plights that are caused by insatiable Napoleonic appetites that too often grossly inspire that sought-after empire shall always tumble down as you're all on Godground. Whenever empires are taken morally unbuilt or taken immorally built, they (the evil formed through free will that sways against God's way) shall always be forsaken empires encoffined to the hilt.

There should never exist any individual shame nor individual blame when sincerely defending your borders against evil's offensive disorder. For there are too many veterans—guardians gallantly drawn—who have died reverently in God's arm.

When humanity is forced to fight, thereby clipping the evil attempting flight, God's heavenly chorus rings expiation. To enforce the sincere defense of evil's offensive disorder requires no further edification when bombs are falling inside your waters. Thee God (Jesus Christ) is specifically referencing the aforesaid to be your United States of America's bloody defensive engagement during World War II.

Although at times appearing displaced, your free will does have its appropriate place. It's a required element for obtaining the results that are befittingly desired for the marvels of human nature itself. God does not control your respective free will; however, free will itself does too many times take control of you.

After you suffer the loss of a dear and beloved family member or friend you presumptuously although duly question: Why would God allow this to happen? Your beyond-painful and agonizing loss unfortunately occurred because free will itself must never truly be disturbed. For only the faithful shall believe in that; thee heavens cry alongside with you.

Free will in all its magnificence of essence is a divinely bestowed luxury that presents for all of you a great deal of responsibility as well as its consequences. It grants you an ability to capture the endless beauty of life itself. Although your choices are plenty, free will dispenses only two paths of entry. By merely assuming our gods' silence, free will itself may appear for the many as totally ungoverned; however, your assumptions may also sound a presuming position of eminence and overconfidence.

As your pharmaceutical industries grind, corporations and their assembly lines are helping to create an evermore displaced human race, synthetically equipped to chemically restructure your neurotransmitter trips. Moreover, prescriptions are being written by too many doctors who sometimes incorporate unnecessary chemical blockers. This newly found pharmacology revolution is sublimating pill-popping solutions at alarming rates, providing the end user that now trades themselves for becoming much more than the abuser and all the while many are masking their more relevant emotional states. When you lock or unblock crucial chemical amino acid chains, there are many caveats to consider throughout your neurotransmitter brains. In stifling these natural occurrences across their natural currents of emotion and thought, you must also begin to consider other plausible disturbances causing these imbalances of emotion and thoughts—traveling amid those too many chemically unequal swaps. And you advertise more and more, as if patients should always self-diagnose because there is always a magic antidote.

Whatever the manufacturer claims, redirecting amino acid chains should not become your children's claim to fame. Much too often, your eminence and prouder unnatural attempts to soften sadness or pain leads some of you into a much louder addictive plead that is becoming more difficult to sustain. Some parents, as well as some doctors, are creating a new devolution consisting of pill-covered tables with too many medicinal staples, conveying to children that if you're unable to cope there are medical antidotes. By being over-prescribed antipsychotic drugs, too many of you are not exploring other possibilities of activity that sur-round more natural hubs of emotional and thought mobility. Your medical community is diagnosing a new disorder yearly. Suddenly humanity needs all the help it can possibly receive in order to function and think more clearly. It's imperative for each you to understand that hardships can also form their prospering partnerships with God, family, yourself, and friends. Pharmacology was indeed created by God to serve many purposes; however, there are some you who *need* and too many of you who just *feed*.

Your displaced eminence and egos, when left unchecked, can easily cast their narcissistic shad-ows that may move you into the immoralities that only become darker whenever your basic morals, values, and principles become too neglected. When you begin believing you're better than all the rest, walking can display the arrogance that slants only your (individual) direction toward self-serving quests. Egos that are overly nourished increase appetites for control with an unyielding persistence that's not easily discouraged. The more egos become generously self-inflated, the further your eminence becomes overly persuaded. It's only through humil-ity if you're able to individually and sincerely attain that the sudden presence of eminence shall rapidly become drained. Do bear in mind, however, that the marvels of human nature are more than just kind when egos do not blind.

Displaced gratification for the millennial generation is evolving into revolving forms of self-serving concentrations. The sources of your pleasure can be a plethora. One must always carefully measure their outcome as well as their invitation. Temptation's invited guests, if overlooked, have a propensity for overbooking their many requests. If you're unable to find your fill through the gratifying pleasures you freely choose to fulfill, sins replace sins that never still. Whatever the sources of temptation may deceivably portray, the gratification you receive may return for you alternate courses that turn to further enforce your sinful sway. Desires do ignite the necessary fires that encourage the soul and takes its altruistic growth ever hirer; however, it's your cravings that guide either the calling or the forestalling of sincere or perhaps insincere desire.

It's evident that your displaced decadence continues widening across your generational gaps, opening wider spaces morally, as some of you are filling their empty places with the immorality that quickly adapts. Attempting to remove prayer when you break to make church and state separate affairs is a religious freedom being more and more pushed in attempts to snuff out prayer, and is quite simply, although slowly, turning out of control—threatening to become dead air. A moment to philosophically reflect on the fact that churches and temples are built in all fifty of the United States, yes? Are some of you therefore attempting to eventually remove not only prayer but also slowly attempting to remove each church and temple from each of their states as well as from your children's classroom air?

If true, perhaps some of you radically few would be better off focusing on how to make schools and states more separate affairs too? For the philosophy here is plain: Without school you'd probably not even be able to write the many laws some of you attempt to radically ordain. The many laws of sages' bygone are slowly being destroyed as some of your radical days prolong. Again, your free will entitles all of you to build or destroy. Humankind may just find itself also rebuilding everything that only you (a displaced human race) have globally, and freely, destroyed.

Removing a child's religious or spiritual foundation inside their classroom and around their dinner tables precariously turns their tables of moral orientation. Through continuously separating the basic morals within biblical binds and all globally recognized major belief systems, while neglecting what your forefathers and God had in mind, only unwinds a generation void of morality and the integrity of associating those fidelities that are spiritually invigorating. Atheists may remain skeptic; however, religious freedoms should always remain a free will election (an act of choosing or the fact of being chosen especially by the masses influence) and only through its exposure offers for humankind the many choices for people to eventually find. As for those smaller groups attempting to disrespectfully undo, again and again, humankind appears to be neglecting its history—globally as well as biblically. And must oftentimes be reminded that you are all living upon Godground.

Your pornography is now an acclaimed billion-dollar industry promoting debauchery and condoning adultery. For they (the evil formed through free will that sways against God's way) decided pornography was just not enough and have now adulterated children for child pornography leaving their victims scarred and defiled. These hedonistic portrayals prey on the morally weak through, stoking desires behind Satanist fibers. Pleasure-driven societies and their embarking dynasties eventually collapse or even vanish due to their diabolic and sickening atrocities. The decadence pornography entices and promotes is increasing your bizarre vices as their oglers flock and evil shops.

One of your history's most evil and sadistic predators, Ted Bundy, blamed pornography as an ill-guided leader.

There is a devolution occurring from within humankind and there are evermore present and disturbing behavioral patterns emerging. All around your principles are fading and all around your decadence is escalating. Some fathers are molesting their sons and daughters as *some* of the ordained are crossing into pedophilia—uncrossing sacred Godground altars. Evil's predatory impostors are registering a new outbreak of their malevolent intake. Instead of *making*, you're evermore simply *taking*—whether its sex, drugs, or money. These are becoming the most sought-after objects with all the evil's usual immoral subjects viewing other people only as targets. Inside pleasure's decadent dome, there shall always reside a caveat of stimulation that's seeking corrupter invitations that roam to eventually destroy people's lives and homes.

As the end days for all of they (evil) draw nearer and clearer, a new reality for all of you (a displaced human race) shall sooner or later appear. The hellish voids that were once occupied by evil souls God cast aside are now forever destroyed (decimated) and, therefore, no longer hellishly, repetitiously incarcerated. Your new reality shall come with great sacrifice as the human race shall too remain, as you already are and have been, responsible for its own posterity. Although humankind may continue to devolve, you may also rest in knowing that evil was never permitted to be involved upon Godground at all. For they (the evil formed through free will that sways against God's way) were given more than ample opportunities to worship God. If they (evil) so badly want to worship and follow Satan, then God (thee Father almighty), our gods, and thee God (Jesus Christ) shall be creating those worshiping alters of Satan soon.

When Godground begins to shake, you (a displaced human race and children of God) shall become holier awake. In this new beginning, evil will suffer a punishing end as Judgment Day has already slowly begun. Relevantly foretold, new beginnings shall unfold with a Godly surge. New worlds and realities shall appear and emerge with some of God's presence globally observed!

And no, you will not remain in human form to inhabit the earth forever. And no, there will be no alien invasion to take over your planet. And no, you will not all just vanish and go away. Only they (evil) shall go away. For Saint Michael thee archangel is incarnated and upon Godground.

Heed thee clear understanding in you (a displaced human race and children of God) already knowing that God (thee Father almighty), our gods, and thee God (Jesus Christ) are the definitive and final judges and jury of they (the evil that only temporarily resides inside, what paths free will provides). This should not surprise you nor shock you. With all of your creeds that exist globally.

~

CHAPTER THREE

THEY
(THE EVIL THAT ONLY TEMPORARILY RESIDES INSIDE, WHAT PATHS FREE WILL PROVIDES)

L ong before your (a displaced human race) Ted Bundy charmers and your Jeffrey Dahmers (the evil that only temporarily resides inside, what paths free will provides), they (evil) were always cast into hell's repetitive chase with the devil.

They are not created by God; evil is only temporarily manifested (as you unfortunately do observe occasionally) through the free will individually quested. Although God creates each and every one of you, one must also command responsibility for their free will that fundamentally shapes you. Your recorded and darker historical known prolific evil personified killers and dictators were all granted numerous opportunities to serve many alternate purposes, other than the darker paths they (evil) freely chose aboard wayward surfaces.

Your many endless opportunities, as well as life's sacred responsibilities, offers only two paths of certainties—an infinite footpath with God or a hellish racepath with the devil that only renders a decimating aftermath. God creates both paths.

This book provides many reoccurring themes you must heed to awaken: God (thee Father almighty), our gods, and thee God (Jesus Christ) created your (a displaced human race's) fictional character Satan and of all its dark symbolic narratives that you've mistakenly taken to blatant extremes. If you believe in all of God's magnificence, then you must ask: What is the significance for such a divine being to therefore create malevolence?

Again, allow yourselves a moment for reflecting upon the following: If one person were to be given the opportunity to live out the remainder of their life upon the surface of the moon, where on earth would this evil loom? Consider another proposed image that requires a much quieter (and only phil-osophical) reflection. If everything on Godground remained, yet humankind suddenly disappeared, would God or this fictional character Satan cease to exist? Once humankind is able to see its way past these clearly misconstrued symbolic good-versus-evil inhibitions, you (a displaced human race) shall begin to indeed realize that God (thee Father almighty), our gods, and thee God (Jesus Christ) creates all, including your fictional character Satan, as well as hell's ascriptions.

The scattering of scorn throughout religious empires that have formed stripped God's biblical validity, leaving many stories confusingly revised through the free will of humankind and its past selectivity. And by doing so, this concealed from humanity the truer and deeper content that eventually unto humankind became greatly overshadowed. Of their too many examples, thee God (Jesus Christ) shall refer to one of its most absurd samples: No God would ever request a child (Isaac), nor any creature, to be purposefully sacrificed in order to appease God. It's of these sorted and contorted overwrites that divest your internal and external Godly insights. The story of your Adam and Eve tasting those forbidden fruits were simply your free will being set afoot, as well as temptation's hook being symbolically introduced. Furthermore, it's because of examples such as these that cause and obscure for too many of you the true nature of God and reality. Throughout your major religiosity trees, leave too many complacently uninquiring while deciphering scriptures individually as your free will does deem appropriate to appease.

The story of Lucifer's (Satan's) shock and fall is, for too many of you, the most overly exaggerated symbolic fictional tale of all—albeit extremely philosophical. The meaning of this story that most of humanity has exacerbated to deliver unto itself the most ludicrous detail: Lucifer's (philosophic and symbolic) representation was nothing more than a simple attribution intended to illustrate that even the most devout followers of God or Christ are capable of falling from grace, alongside those many available routes inside your human free will traits.

When you (a displaced human race) reference figuratively transposed passages biblically, please do not ignore thee God's (Jesus Christ's) proposed inference subjectively by taking to therefore compose, or impose, their verses too literally. Within your reality, they (evil) do occasionally appear; however, understanding the difference between something that is created versus manifested, once again, is your (individual) free will's profound significance.

For those of you who feel, you must allow for Lucifer's fictional overemphasis. By doing so, are you missing God's reverence? Lucifer's metaphorical entry has incited your many religious platforms,

THEY   71

at times with an overly exaggerated provocative intensity. Furthermore, in the process there is a relevant irony for all of you to observe: Satan's fictional depiction has no attributes other than what's drawn from your individual conviction. From all the symbolic tales that you've twisted leading you to believe that Satan ever existed. If this were truly the case, all of God's creations would be in vain as well as isolated from God's beyond-infinite perfection and grace.

It's only whereof God (thee Father almighty), our gods, and thee God (Jesus Christ) that all life, and omnipotence for duly having a God-complex, that all above and beyond-infinite life has originated and is divinely delegated. Believing a fictional character such as Satan inhabits the earth is a total contradiction of what formed humankind's birth. How can some of you think that two extremely opposing forces such as God and your fictional character Satan could both exist and *coexist*? No matter your religious stature, you must begin questioning: How does this Lucifer manage to hide so incredibly well? While eluding God's (thee Father almighty's), our gods', and thee God's (Jesus Christ's) capture?

The evil you (a displaced human race) temporarily see manifested is occurring because of free will only. Moreover, in allowing all life to freely flourish, free will exemplifies the intrinsic attributes for the marvels of human nature amid what God, our gods, and thee God so lovingly and graciously distribute.

Once pure evil is formed, the soul undeniably darkens becoming too spiritually deformed. God does not forgive all. If that were the case, that would create nothing more than a paradoxical pitfall for all of humanity and your Godly provided belief systems. This now becomes a wonderful example, and perhaps for some of you this is all an epiphany in knowing exactly why God is God and you're just you (a precious and displaced human race). God (thee Father almighty), our gods, and thee God (Jesus Christ) are your creators as well as your decimators of all evil spirits. And just as a reminder, thee God does have a God-complex because God is beyond-infinitely complex indeed.

Evil cults use biblical verses for their preying purposes. Borrowing scripture and too many times totally creating their own newly devised belief systems or ideologies. Then these evil cult leaders isolate their following with manipulative biblical narratives for an ulterior calling as they (the evil that only temporarily resides inside, what paths free will provides) more than violate those precious Godly seekers. These types of manipulators, unfortunately, exemplify your too many dogmatic combinations that are being used and abused to unlock profuse religious variations, which in turn lock spirituality and block your factuality. Such distorted religious pulpits of manmade evil culprits are extending their ludicrous markets, through the sale of betrayal, as their people become unmindful puppets, patronizing God in its process—behind evil's façade. These evil cults seemingly have the ability to somehow always manage to find their followers' weaker faults, eventually turning their supporters' isolation into extreme desperation. Using their nefarious efforts to discredit other unmindful members and their mindsets sets in motion for the evil cult, the notion that in order for their members to have or feel complete devotion that it can only be acknowledged through their followers individual obedience and loyalty to their cult leaders—not God. This slowly creates an urgency for their members or followers to ostracize their family and friends, as well as to aggrandize their cult leaders.

Evil sects are notoriously adept as they (the evil that only temporarily resides inside, what paths free will provides) redirect the good toward evil in order to control and manipulate their subjects gradually in a more nefarious way. For they (evil) are deceivers with only one wicked purpose—to connect with their believers for evil's purpose. Too many of your distorted religious pulpits arise from the highest of unholy culprits.

Popular threads for evil cults and evil sects are to sow, and they (evil) do eventually reap, through selling you beliefs by way of overlapping their trust and using it as a technique to induce your individual or group guilt which is often what they seek. For example, leading you to believe that you cannot become totally committed to serving their cult leader's eminent façade, not necessarily God, although they tell you they are somehow serving a deity of some variety unless you once again ostracize your family, friends and perhaps even society. And by making you feel beyond guilty for being just you, a moment of reflection concerning this very matter: You must question these evil leaders and their past, how have they lived and what exactly have they done that has made them more special than you in the eyes of God? Furthermore, they enjoy restricting you from exploring any and all other belief systems and their spiritual or religious alternatives. If you do not adhere to their mindset that their way is the only way, you shall feel the wrath of their cult leaders and their committed brainwashed members too, but not necessarily that of God. These are all common staples found upon the darkest tables.

Your liberation becomes invigoration, so they say; however, the very core for any evil cult or evil sect is manipulation that centers throughout their beyond stringent rules and regulations as your family ties soon become outsiders to then chastise. And then the growing pains of these family members who are left feeling abandoned and rejected become eventually more strained and negatively affected. However, do reflect on this simple philosophic additive: There is a clear (obvious) distinction between evil versus obsession. Meaning these members and followers alike do become a bit preoccupied (obsessed) with their cult or sect leaders and their founders.

Now, some your sociologists may very well argue these sects-versus-cults issues and their past similarity within how Christianity originally formed. Just to clarify the obvious for all of you, your various Godly provided belief systems that were discussed in Chapter One have been around for thousands of years prior to any of your science of sociology as well as their forefathers and all of you (a precious and displaced human race).

In practicing your many improvisations of their too many doctored doctrines of variations, some of you are devotionally unraveling alongside your baby carriages strolling inside too many barricaded marriages. Meanwhile, as some of you doctrinally imbibe alongside an improperly held Bible Belt, it morally unbuckles. Hedonism develops as debauchery begins to buckle some of you. When exactly did polygamy suddenly become a comparable or justifiable lifestyle of holy entry? Or is this perhaps an excuse for the abuse of adultery? The hypocrisy pelted toward the gospels you've dealt with loosen around some of your Bible Belts as these manipulative founders and leaders tighten their grip alongside bigamy and gelt (money).

These too many humankind self-drafted belief systems, inside their self-serving amenities, are indeed becoming an extremely broken dichotomy of divinities. Some of your Bible-imbibing arrivals and so-called biblical groups are becoming quite ridiculous displays that are increasingly resembling their chutes of more Neanderthal days. Furthermore, by performing these onstage exorcism dramatics and snake handlers' antics, it appears some of your religious demographics have reached their lowest status. Perhaps some of you require a brief journey of reverse forensics regarding the use of your religious and spiritual lenses? Or just perhaps at this point in your reading, revisit Chapter One?

Although bad can at times lean on evil, distinguishing their differences entails its own significance.

These bad-versus-evil distinctions can become easily interlaid, resulting in a dangerous moral interplay. Inside evil's temporary formation are disturbing progressions of flawed immoral gradations. Although at times belated, bad may quickly become inflated and, therefore, temporarily manifest itself into hatred wherefrom your bad adulthood behavior versus evil becomes indiscernibly conflated.

By taking oneself beyond the most basic of sinful levels, you penetrate those paths that are only taken by your philosophical devils. There are sins God considers plausibly acceptable as these are parts of growth that are perhaps correctable. Being a bad person does not necessarily, nor fairly, correlate to an evil counterpart version or assertion. The further one moves toward scandalous directions, the further one is only creating for themselves possibly a precursor into more nefarious connections. Each of you are given ample opportunity to grow as well as learn what each individual soul yearns for. This will eventually mold your inner being as your free will guides its moral or immoral turns. The soul when created is pure; it's of your own free will that carries only two paths and you (a precious and displaced human race) also control the direction for either a Godly reflection or nefarious lure.

Some of you believe that God (thee Father almighty), our gods, and thee God (Jesus Christ) for whatever reason eventually forgive evil, but once they (evil) have died forgiveness is not something for the unwise to unjustly surmise. Whenever blood spills, wherein evil murders and kills, it's the intentional position that sets it completely apart from its unintentional disposition. This aforesaid concerning evil was already known, yes? Within your plenty concepts of heaven and hell? So this should be a pansophy (considered certainly by now to be more of humankind knowledge rather than its defined universal knowledge) perhaps? Was thee God (Jesus Christ) crucified to include the forgiveness of they (evil)? If so, then you (humankind) are all in a much more serious devolution and extremely troubling as well as undiscerning conceptional fall.

When the taking of another precious life is unintentionally committed, there are specific mortal consequential concessions that our gods may have permitted, providing *some* justly redemptions. For example, when it concerns sincere self-defense—and *not* unjust offense—you may sincerely fight for your own precious plight; however, do not straddle its philosophical fence. For this next proceeding statement is worth more than just reflecting upon: When saints and angels are forced into evil's war, fighting does then become necessary, although extremely hostile, and much more than a blood-shedding and individually changing chore.

As one may so shrewdly attempt to straddle his or her moral fence, there are both severe implications as well as rigid indications for the proper use in your self-defense situations. Be wary withal thee Ten Commandments that you individually choose to so righteously vary and then carry out. In defending against evil hostilities, far too many Godly good brave men and woman have gallantly fought and died under flags emboldened with liberty that were justly and defensively carried out.

Being forced to fight in order to take down evil's temporary flight, God does not necessarily celebrate those nor indict hell's decimating throes. Let there be caution beheld inside brutal wars' upheld, when combating what evil has torn, one can become individually changed by that violent outcome of their many battles that were forced and worn. Protecting family as well as country is a hallowed and human characteristic of unity and holy solidarity, for the value of life itself as well as the nature of self-preservation delivers those inherent and necessary obligations. Protecting countries that is, not invading countries!

The commotion of emotion, alongside free will, play their vital roles in whether or not evil temporarily takes an available slot. There is a great deal of danger in your anger, and your frustrations can easily become its instigator. Disappointment may well rearrange anger's appointment. Once inner rage opens its cage, what escapes only evil temporarily relates. Evil's temporary manifestations, although unnatural in their origination, are pitched with emotional rotation.

Be aware that in your life, you're the pilot apace with free will and emotions that rapidly can change within your environment and violently climb in its climate setting your inner compass, living amiably like an apostle, or being hostile as Pontius Pilate.

When jealousies feed and possibly join with greed, evil can arouse with an undaunted (not discouraged or afraid to continue) speed. Jealousy can easily manifest itself into hate by wanting whatever you desire so badly that it initiates your unfounded need to take. You shall always want for that of what you do not have; it's more importantly those methods of obtainment that one may choose to use and draft. Careless love triangles develop jealous entanglements that may lead into darker and more nefarious angles. Extreme jealousy blinds the onset

of sin—offsetting the right from wrong—and may
allow evil to frustratingly spin.

Bigotry shall only take you onto hatred's prec-
ipice. Hate, although an unnatural human trait,
sets itself dangerously forth in motion sometimes
through frustrations' promotion. Furthermore,
once frustrations become overly elevated and
develop into anger, evil is temporarily manifested
from hatred being well baited. You perhaps become
much more persuaded. The greatest danger in your
anger is not knowing that anger panders for its evil
anchors. It's okay to become mad or feel like an
angry absurd bird from time to time; it's knowing the marvels of human nature that this emotion
(being upset) becomes a clear, distinct, and significant difference. For example, being or feeling mad
about something is not necessarily anger, and feeling angry is similar at times to just feeling, or being,
a bit bitter.

If some aforementioned portions in your reading of this divine material appears to be common
sense, bear in mind that it's being written for all of
humankind and not just for you (individually). At
this point do feel ever so free into referring yourself
once again to the back cover of this book.

Those dearly departed souls together with all
victims of hate, God (thee Father almighty), our

gods, and thee God (Jesus Christ) hold dearly inside a spiritual realm. These souls are awaiting their loved ones to accompany them, *only* when God is ready for you to arrive. Enjoy your life and take your time, for suicide is not the answer, as your soul would only depart before it could fully arrive. Know these dearly departed souls and victims of hate shall once again be held by their bonds that God's love has forever created and tied for all of you (a precious and displaced human race).

Evil's hateful eruption can easily become aroused through the introduction of your many artificial seductions. Your harmony can easily sway becoming suggestively strained, leaning toward sin through abusing drugs or alcohol whether prescribed or illegally obtained. When these substances become frequently consumed, the soul now disrupted is more enticingly corrupted in consequence; there becomes an emotional as well as a moral divide. Although it's human nature to feel good, the temporary productions using artificial seductions also yield their definitive repercussions. Evil is notorious for its atrocious delusions of grandeur. Abusing drugs and alcohol amplify this false stature. Your biological chemistry is a complex and delicate synergy, by intentionally murdering and killing then to claim mental insanity fame is an unjustly Godground nonnegotiable plea.

Money is not the root of all evil; it's merely the greed as well as the desire you individually plant throughout its uprooting pursuit. Our gods created your monetary system in order to provide for your human race a functional and structured prosperous rhythm.

Whether they (the evil that only temporarily resides inside, what paths free will provides) were once chosen as subjects of worship, such as your Jim Jones or pontificated anti-Semitism atop Adolf Hitler-alike narcissistic political thrones. These evil spirits that were fragments of hell's clutter are now decimated through the incarnation of Saint Michael's: silent and heavenly Godground invocation.

Hitler is one of your most fundamental examples of how free will can take, then carry, an intended direction into grim kilter. Regardless how evil they (the evil that only temporarily resides inside, what paths free will provides) become, God's original creations are meant for alternative applications. Having inspiration first as an artist, Hitler's vision turned evil's darkest. Hitler was created by God to become a great political leader, shifting Germany's tattered economy not to become the darkest evil your world histories have acknowledged.

Evil's brutality and savagery, throughout cultures such as your Aztec history, are unfortunate traits that still remain within your modern-day displays of sinisterity.

Within all of your belief systems that humankind has designated, the following shall appear abundantly clear as a new understanding becomes globally resonated. Evil is always decimated and never ever tolerated! There is no excuse for the free will they (evil) abuse. In the midst of your free will, there is no granted atonement for choosing to become evil. Our gods do not allow the reincarnation of evil to reintroduce that which God more than rebukes! In believing that God forgives all, you are greatly mistaken, for they (the evil that only temporarily resides inside, what paths free will provides) are more than justly forsaken. For all evil paths there is no escaping God's (thee Father almighty's) hellish impending, and now decimating, wrath.

Just as there does exist a beyond-infinite heavenly source for creating all life, there does also exist a Godly beyond-infinite perpetual natured divine perforce (by force of circumstances or necessity) that indelibly ensures its beyond-infinitely eternal perfection and grace source.

Judgment Day was always upon they (the evil that only temporarily resides inside, what paths free will provides). Welcome all of you (a precious and displaced human race) once again to a familiar title our gods feel for all humankind shall become extremely vital in Godology/Jesusology 101.

CHAPTER FOUR

THEE ARRIVAL
OF SAINT MICHAEL

The morals of humankind are always on trial and are exactly the terms of which turns Armageddon's dial. Humankinds' mounting frustrations as you (a precious and displaced human race) seek Godly divine validations from their assumed and concealed silent locations are now becoming preeminently revealed with God's (thee Father almighty's), our gods', and thee God's (Jesus Christ's) divine proclamation of Saint Michael thee archangel's incarnation.

Thee arrival of Saint Michael fulfills an everlasting archangel course, one our lords of your sphere forewarned as you (a precious and displaced human race) shall now only watch. For they (evil) have always been held more than accountable to God as the profiles of Judgment Day have already began its cycle. Hell's no longer brimming with the evil spirits of mortal sinning, as God's unseen variation of your apocalyptic revelations now unfolds with the beginning of Saint Michael thee archangel's fourth role, already rippling across Godground poles.

Of the many embellished Judgment Day scenarios humanity foreshadowed, it was the simple, philosophical essence of Satan's fictional character as well as your (a precious and displaced human race) good-versus-evil battles that became for humankind a preference unfortunately overshadowed. Saint Michael's creation arose from God's delegations to rid your world of evil. God does not require your fictional battleground representations. When your religious beliefs become suppressions in searching for relief, the lessons for truly understanding God's beyond-infinite framework tend to cease.

The evil spirits that once occupied hell's repetitious abyss are now decimated through God's beyond-infinite perfection and grace and with Saint Michael thee archangel's incarnation of divine bliss. Throughout your religious meetings, you've more than over-polarized your good-versus-evil teachings, treating them with inflated tales that have long lost their origin as well as their truer meaning.

The evil that you see temporarily manifested is in itself temporarily exhibiting the antichrist biblically suggested.

There shall be no antichrist (Satan) reining upon your world: Saint Michael thee archangel's wings are now infinitely and saintly unfurled. Biblical blemishes have portrayed for you (a precious and displaced human race) distorted and fictitious revelational battleground images. Led through heaven, Armageddon is upon Godground as thee fourth horse silently tracks. Our gods shall relax your reality, bringing forth for those who endure God's wrath (you, a precious and displaced human race), peace amid their new world maps.

Divinely set in motion, revelations' mere culmination was inevitably a bloodless invocation and only God creates its Godly surreal presentation. Saint Michael's arc evoked a heavenly spark, inviting thee second coming as four new worlds shall glow and their seven heavenly trumpets will blow. Eternal church bells have been ringing and God (thee Father Almighty), our gods, and thee God (Jesus Christ) have been ringing the tolls of hell for they (evil) for much longer than any of you may actually realize. It was more than wise of you (a precious and displaced human race) to at least not follow the beast. For Saint Michael thee archangel's feast began before any of you, and your forefathers too, ever lived to talk and tell about heaven or hell.

God's beyond-infinite rotations of all creations do indeed have their delegated purposes that infinitely turn to return alongside infinite surfaces of beyond divine combinations. Godborne Saint Michael thee archangel now inhabits human form, marking the gathering of revelation's silent, and infinitely throughout eternity, ever so Holy-storm. Saint Michael's-arc of self-recognition forever transitioned evil's imminent perdition. There is no battleground beyond Godground! Incarnated, Saint Michael in human form only needed to become self-recognized, since evil is only created in human form and by free will sown. Therefore, it's only in human form that God would ever allow Saint Michael thee archangel to become forever evil's decimating storm.

Free will was also bestowed upon Saint Michael thee archangel and shall obviously remain. During the many years prior to Saint Michael being self-aware, his free will could've taken him anywhere.

Just as they (evil) decisively sway, Saint Michael was given plenty of opportunities to go astray, for within his human form the waves of emotion occasionally challenged the free will inside his motion too. It's also within these challenges that enhance your ability to consciously form your inner being, or consciously form the evil you see only temporarily being. Once again, there are only two paths of entry. Does anyone recall these topics being covered within thee Holy Bible? And, throughout the majority of your more popular beliefs that were also discussed inside Chapter One? Perhaps, the awareness of these two paths of entry may appear to be complete common sense then?

Although incomprehensible, God's functionality and form coincides within its omnipotence of beyond infinites coexisting tabula-rasa (something existing in its original pristine state) divine framework drives, guiding thee eternal beyond-infinite divides. Throughout God zones, heavenly trumpets have blared when Saint Michael thee archangel became inherently declared upon Godground and he grew self-aware. Saint Michael's angelic spark ignited God's send and posted heavenly arc to everlastingly assign and align seven into the procession of Armageddon.

God's piloting silence of beyond-infinite divine courses has bridled all four horses; their canter centered upon thee Judgment Day they (evil) have long ago already freely entered. Godground is for all a palace, and Godground for all shall thunder with gallops as Godground will soon cease of all its malice.

As humankind so often becomes blinded, humanity must too often be reminded that all life is Godly presided over and God is in charge of all life as well as its beyond-infinite order. Whenever decadent lifestyles reach a more acceptable place, malevolence usually appears in haste, such as was the turn of your (humankind's) twentieth-century pace. Furthermore, there are many peering correlations within some of your divine deviations that have all of humankind possibly unaware that you've all been steering toward revelations.

Our gods of beyond-infinitely limitless creations have removed many of your (humankind's) lost civilizations. When humankind begins to climb with a false sense of eminence and power, God will surely show you the way back down that tower. Outside your good-versus-evil superficial fight, our gods decimated the evil spirits that were inside hell where they (the evil formed through free will that sways against God's way) were always cast repetitiously tight. God's wrath upon only they (evil) is a bloodless path indeed.

Understanding what is truly good would not be possible without unveiling what's evil; therefore, Satan's fictional character was introduced as a necessary and revealing philosophical subject. That subject perhaps became a bit too real in the mindsets of some of your own unfortunate misreading.

These many lost directives and their philosophical/symbolic directions of diction are what cost humankind great loss amid your struggles of understanding our gods' beyond-infinite collective divine cause. Because God is all loving, there is a divine complexity for humanity's clarity. Evil is not created by God; evil spirits, however, are decimated by God.

Saint Michael thee archangel, though incarnated, shall never be recognized in his physical form nor perform as a prophet upon any stage alongside your Godly blessed religious/spiritual platforms. And, by anyone claiming to be Saint Michael thee archangel shall indeed fall if ever attempting to stand that tall! Now as he walks with great humility upon Godground, Saint Michael shall never be adorned by any fanfare nor crown. Thee seven seals have opened and with Godground in a state of despair, God shall perhaps repair? Just how God will do this is a responsibility for all of humanity too share. How humankind decides to respond is real and within your own free will. Of great concern is if you (a precious and displaced human race) must totally relearn?

You have for centuries been involved in battles consisting of nothing more than greed and your own religious concerns and needs. Your own powerplay is something God may just take away. God is watching—our gods and thee God (Jesus Christ) are concerned. Godground may just continue to burn especially if you must relearn regarding your bloody and violent history that hides behind no mystery.

If humankind does rather choose to not listen, new worlds shall either glisten or you shall be replaced back into your once: Neanderthal place! Thee signs have slowly been turning and yet have arrived clearly described—there is a battle, if you will, of good versus evil. However, the good is all around you every day and every night. This evil you occasionally see is only temporarily exhibited and ultimately was always Godly prohibited.

God (thee Father almighty), our gods, and thee God (Jesus Christ) are your lords of Godground, and they (evil) have clearly chosen their free will paths. God did not ever convey any mercy for they (evil). Sins are perhaps forgiven; however, pure evil's gravest of sins after they die are never forgiven. If this were so, then what are your concepts of heaven and hell, and why do these beliefs even exist in your world? Once again, these topics were briefly discussed in Chapter One concerning your major religions and belief systems. Atheists and agnostics, you may continue remaining skeptical. Upon Godground you may very well apply the use of free will, although this does not necessarily also imply for you (humankind) to exert the use of free rein. Animals do, however, have free rein.

Once Saint Michael thee archangel became aware of his true being, a Godforce advent surged, setting forth a Godly indelible and unconditional divine reconvening. As is mentioned on the back cover of this book, there must, as you know, be an end to something in order to begin anew. Judgement Day is on God's time and not that of mankind. Upon Godground, the wings of Saint Michael thee archangel are now infinitely opened and shall infinitely flutter. As the calling of old worlds close, the dawning of a new world shall expose God's everlasting glory as humankind enters into a Godly brighter and newer territory.

Saint Michael's book of love is a story—although untold, shall now be read and the truth for all of humankind will eventually unfold. Heavenly trumpets blare as Saint Michael thee archangel's angelic presence is now upon Godground inside and outside God's light of white glare, where God's army (saints and angels) now everlastingly preside.

God thanks all of you for praying and remaining patient in your awaiting for some kind of sign (any sign). God was listening. Were there any real doubts of that? God wants all of you to continue enjoying your precious gifts of life together with family, friends and partners alike. If you feel like dancing, dance; if you feel like rejoicing, rejoice. And if you feel like praying, pray. Its okay to let yourself go and have fun. For the marvels of human nature are all around you today and tomorrow too.

~

ABOUT THE AUTHOR

VIC T. FARLEY is not a literary scholar nor prophet. We all have our own unique relationships with God, faith, religion, and their belief systems/credos.

There is no wrong or right way to find that individual connection we globally seek with God, or whatever higher power you (individually) conceive or perceive to be God.

My journey in life has been one of extraordinary beauty, pain, internal struggles, sadness, personal loss, and at times a great deal of frustration. However, I always turned to God for comfort throughout those difficult and trying times. For I, just like you and so many other people in this challenging world of ours, also had my own plan. Many of which were born of my dreams while some were inspired by other people that've so blessedly crossed my path, leaving behind their inspiring traces and long-lasting soul shine.

Many times throughout my life, I felt that I was truly being saved. Then, and with enduring introspection, I'd personally question: Why am I being saved? For I'm struggling just like everyone else with trying to find my place in this life. And although I often felt complicated on the inside and misunderstood on the outside, still I made every possible effort to maintain a simple level of humility. I used to often say that it's interesting how similar we all are and yet at the same time so completely different individually. Thank God my feelings have never changed in knowing that I'm just me, and you are just you. And that our individuality is exactly what helps to shape our personalities and the many experiences that we blessedly share with those around us.

I consider myself a simple and unassuming man. I'm not a famous actor, musician, artist, nor author.

Ever since I can remember, I've always believed that God has a plan for all of us, and that whatever you seek in your dreams—as well as the inspiration you find from others—you shall sooner or later discover and further develop that plan with the help and guidance of true faith.

I also believe some of the most significant examples of success in our world are made by those who work two or three jobs in order to provide for their loved ones. These wonderful people are making difficult sacrifices all out of love for their families and helping to turn the pages of real success stories that are happening each and every day all around us. Their stories unfortunately too often go unrecognized.

After many years of struggling to find my way in various jobs and silly titles that were given to me, I felt defeated, in that no matter what amount of effort I put forth into finding a career and educating myself at local community colleges, it just seemed at times as if my life was destined to become filled with many jobs and empty of any sought-after career. However, I always remained optimistic about eventually finding that company somewhere on the horizon that would eventually have an opening career position for me to fulfill my long-anticipated climb aboard its corporate ladder. During my search I considered starting up my own business. After consistently feeling career blocked, it became clear to me that my plan was not nearly as significant as the plan God had for me.

Bringing this material forward with Jesus Christ has been a personal journey of enormous beauty as well as joy. This divine journey and experience with Jesus Christ undoubtedly invigorated me; however, there were many times I thought, felt, and believed that through safeguarding this book's material that I may very well be taking this material to my grave before it's ever published.

As the author and publisher of this divine material, I believe that God is disenchanted with the human race and greatly concerned about the direction in which humankind is traveling. I further believe God smiles upon each and every one of us whenever we are kind and caring to one another or whenever we open our hands and hearts to sincerely help someone less fortunate than ourselves.

That help can be as simple as sharing a friendly smile or a kind word with someone who you may not necessarily desire to share it with or as small as giving a few dollars to help another less fortunate to feed themselves or their child—even if it's only just for a moment.

www.ingramcontent.com/pod-product-compliance
Lightning Source LLC
Chambersburg PA
CBHW031628040426
42452CB00007B/723